MW01232497

MANIPULATION AND PERSUASION

The Ultimate Guide to Understand the Art of the Most Powerful
Persuasion Tactics and Mind Control Techniques

By

Jake Bishops

Table of Contents

Introduction

Persuasion refers to using communication deliberately to change, form, or strengthen people's attitudes, the last-mentioned being mental representations that outline what we think about things, people, groups, actions, or ideas: if we prefer one brand to another, if we are for or against abortion, what we think about certain political parties, etc.

Since attitudes play an important role in the way we behave, a significant change in them should lead to a change in our behavior, which is what persuasion is really about. For example, we may want people to buy a particular product from us, to stop smoking, to wear a seat belt, or to give us their vote in elections.

Having the teenagers evaluate the parking area as something unpleasant (negative attitude) also made them behave accordingly. To persuade is to encourage others to voluntarily accept our way of seeing things and to respect, cherish, and take into account our approaches.

We can influence another person by our way of being and acting, but the one who influences can do it almost unconsciously; on the other hand, the one who persuades does intend that the other person's opinion be changed and wishes that the one who assumes his or her positions does so of his or her own accord and making use of his or her freedom of choice.

How to Communicate in a Persuasive Way

Persuasion is not technically brainwashing but is rather the manipulation of the human mind by some other individual, without the manipulated individual being aware of whatever caused their change of mind. The basis of persuasion always works to access the right side of your brain. The left side of your brain is analytical and rational. The right side is creative and imaginative. It is overly simplified, but it explains my point. Therefore, to distract the left side of the brain and keep it busy is the idea.

© Copyright 2021 by Jake Bishops - All rights reserved.

Chapter 1: The Art of Persuasion - NLP

Perhaps you were considering being hypnotized yourself and you wanted to know more about the process. Or maybe you have always considered a career in psychology, in particular, hypnotherapy.

Many people wonder if hypnosis can be used to persuade people—to win arguments, negotiate purchases and sell people things, and so on. The truth is that hypnosis truly is meant to be a therapy. That is, the field of hypnosis originated with psychologists whose goal was to help people change undesirable attitudes, fears, and behaviors. With hypnotherapy, a therapist can delve deep into a person's subconscious and reprogram how that person thinks and reacts in their waking state.

Yet there are other ways to use the subconscious.

Hypnotherapy uses several different techniques. Among these are the ideas of mirroring and leading, strategies that are part of another area of psychological study called neuro-linguistic programming, or NLP, as it is commonly called. NLP is a method of changing how we communicate with others to create more favorable outcomes for ourselves and those we communicate with. That is, if you understand NLP you better understand how people think and behave, and you better understand how to have productive interactions with people—interactions that accomplish goals, both yours and theirs.

We will talk briefly about NLP, teaching you a few concepts that you can use in your everyday life to have more beneficial interactions with other people. You can also use these tips if you go into hypnosis practice to build a better rapport with your subjects and to best help them achieve their goals.

NLP is a way of reading body language and mood and using this information to lead the other person where you want them to go. When you properly implement NLP, you can communicate better with your partner, be a better parent, work better with your colleagues, communicate more effectively with your boss, and more. When you learn NLP, you learn to know yourself better, to read what other people are thinking, and to have a direct impact on the world.

Psychologists and laypeople have used the practice of NLP for decades. Somewhat similar to hypnosis, NLP is both an art and a science, an idea that is founded on sound observation and research, yet a skill that is developed through practice and mindfulness. Put simply, NLP is a type of subconscious programming (just like hypnosis!); it's something that we all exhibit every day. For example, if someone says something that upsets you, you may subconsciously tighten your jaw and your body muscles, staying very still as you process the information.

This is a subconscious response, part of our fight-or-flight tendencies, which first tell your body to freeze as you access a situation.

Many therapists use NLP techniques in counseling their clients, as NLP can be a very effective way to manage phobias and anxiety. NLP counseling can also help people who have had a difficult past (perhaps with abuse or trauma) to move on and learn to manage their memories. NLP has been used by dating coaches to help instill confidence in their clients and by marketing professionals to better reach their target markets. NLP can also be used on one'sself in a very simple way but with profound outcomes. Let's look ata few of the most fundamental NLP concepts, and how you canusethis subconscious programming to benefit you and others in everyday life.

NLP has been used in alternative medicine to treat illnesses like Parkinson's disease. It has also been used in psychotherapy, advertisement, sales, management, coaching, teaching, team building, and public speaking. Yes, each one of these categories is a form of manipulation to some degree. You can't go to a class, the grocery store, or even a restaurant without being subject to some form of manipulation. No matter where you are, you can't escape it. It's present in advertisement posters, the tactic of that business sales clerk that stops you at the mall, the product placement in the movie you're watching, and everywhere else. However, instead of being afraid of this knowledge, you can use it to your advantage and redirect that manipulation as the wielder.

But some skilled individuals can harness this power to give them an unbeatable advantage. The techniques are best used in a one-on-one or small group environment. The fewer people involved, the easier it is to read and apply NLP methods.

NLP is a complex subject and is often taught over years. That's because it takes practice to learn the range of reactions people can express. But the promise of learning people's inner secrets makes this technique especially attractive to con artists and law enforcement.

A skilled NLP user can determine:

Which Side of the Brain Their Subject Uses?

People fall along a spectrum between creative and analytical. New science shows that brain function is distributed across the brain. But it is still helpful to think of people through this lens.

Word choice, sentence structure, and associations all reveal details about the person that uses them. Left-brained people often use words that elicit emotions or experiences. Right-brained people like to include things outside their experience or expertise.

Which Sense Is Most Important to Them?

We have more than the five senses (sight, sound, taste, touch, and smell) most people know about. We also have a sense of order, balance, morality, and a host of others, and each of us has one or two that are more important than the rest.

How Their Brain Stores Information

Our brains are the most complex computers we have ever come across. They store and process billions of bits of information for a second. Each one functions a little differently. One of the biggest areas of divergence is in how people store information.

Some individuals have a memory like a sponge, soaking up everything near them. Others are more like a filter that catches big chunks and allows everything to pass through. NLP techniques help people discern the difference and to what degree.

Over time, NLP users get better at keeping track of information. With enough time, users can improve their information tracking abilities to near-genius levels. This gives us an advantage over anyone who isn't as experienced or naturally gifted.

When They Are Lying or Making Things Up

People perform specific behaviors when they make things up called "tells." NLP users like me can pick up on these tells and be able to call out the liar as they lie. Some people are better than others at lying, but everyone has at least one tell.

Skilled liars understand that for someone else to believe their lie, so must they. So they convince themselves of it first. They often don't display all the signs of dishonesty because they truly believe the lie as they tell it.

Practice can help people fall for their lies, but the process demands a selective memory. This feature is more reliably detected than the oft-cited slight downward glance. It also proves to be a more consistent indicator of ingrained deception than awkward looks. Power imbalances also make a refusal to make eye contact less reliable as well.

How to Make Someone Drop Their Guard

When someone likes you, they want to include you in their lives. Listening to what they say often provides deep insight into what controls their lives. People offer up their darkest secrets willingly, believing that I truly understand them.

How You Can Condition People Without Their Consent/Knowledge

Let's face it; people don't like finding out someone was manipulating them. It violates the idea that we are in control of our lives. But sometimes the truth is hard to take, and we need someone to help us see the way without calling us out on it.

We all manipulate those around us to one degree or another. This can be as simple as breaking a bad habit or establishing new relationship rules with a toxic family member. By steering them in the right direction, we can help them respond to how we prefer.

NLP doesn't brainwash someone (that's covered elsewhere) or cause them to do something out of character. But it does reveal the strings that control each of us. What you do with those strings once you have them is up to you.

Listen and Watch

This is the most time-consuming step, as it is the basis of building the structure for the more intimate relationship you'll build later. Body language is essential to NLP practices. Not only is it vital to the beginning, but knowing how to read body language comes into play throughout the NLP process and any other psychological process. Luckily, the longer you build a relationship with someone, the easier it will be to know they tell, as they are developed from habit. Some people may be guarded around you, which will appear as tense or straight shoulders and back, not holding your gaze, or even fidgeting. This is a sign you aren't building a vital rapport. Before moving any further, this person needs to feel relaxed and warm around you. Watch for an open face, a relaxed smile, and some easy-going interaction such as light laughter. Stay away from heavy topics until this person is comfortable with you.

Building Rapport with Others

Every day we use our communications to try and influence others. Unfortunately, most of us are rarely successful because we don't know what we are doing—we don't understand the psychology of other people. We don't know how to get into another person's subconscious mind.

One important aspect of getting on well with others is the building of rapport. First, let's consider what rapport is. Rapport is simple, it is the magic that happens when two people are getting along really well and communicating on the same level. When you have a rapport with another person, you are each understanding the other; you are listening better, and you are accomplishing something.

You do not have to think the same way as another person or agree with everything they say to have rapport. You simply have to be communicating similarly. One way that people show rapport is when they mirror each other, that is to say, they have similar body language. People who have a good rapport use similar body language, including posture and eye contact. Imagine in your head that you are talking and laughing with a friend. Likely, you are both standing with your feet a comfortable width apart, your arms moving animatedly as you speak, you are both smiling, and your eyes make frequent contact.

Chapter 2: Persuasion and Influence

There are many times when the human mind is pretty easy to influence, but it does take a certain set of skills to get people to stop and listen to you. Not everyone is good with influence and persuasion, though. They can talk all day and would not be able to convince others to do what they want. On the other hand, some could persuade anyone to do what they want, even if they had just met this person for the first time. Knowing how to work with these skills will make it easier for you to recognize a manipulator and be better prepared to avoid them if needed.

The first thing that we need to look at is what persuasion is. Persuasion is simply the process or action taken by a person or a group of people when they want to cause something to change. This could be with another human being and something that changes in their inner mental systems or their external behavior patterns.

The act of persuasion, when it is done properly, can sometimes create something new within the person, or it can just modify something already present in their minds. Three different parts come with the process of persuasion including:

- The communicator or other source of the persuasion.
- The persuasive nature of the appeal.

- The audience or the target person of the appeal.

All three elements must be taken into consideration before you try to do any form of persuasion on your own. You can just look around at the people who are in your life, and you will probably be able to see some types of persuasion happening all over the place.

The above options are all positive ways that you can use persuasion to your advantage. Most people will be amenable to these happening. But on the other side, there are four negative tactics of persuasion that you can do as well. These would include options like manipulating, avoiding, intimidating, and threatening. These negative tactics will be easier for the target to recognize, which is why most manipulators will avoid using them if possible.

Now, you can use some of the tactics above. Still, according to psychologist Robert Cialdini, six major principles of persuasion can help you to get the results that you want without the target being able to notice what is going on. Let us take a look at some of the weapons and how they can be effective.

Weapons of Persuasion
Reciprocity

The first principle of persuasion that you can use is known as reciprocity. This is based on the idea that when you offer something to someone, they will feel a bit indebted to you and will want to reciprocate it back. Humans are wired to be this way to survive. For the manipulator to use this option, they will make sure that they are doing some kind of favor for their target. Whether that is paying them some compliments, giving them a ride to work, helping out with a big project, or getting them out of trouble. Once the favor is done, the target will feel like they owe a debt to the manipulator. The manipulator will then be able to ask for something, and it will be really hard for the target to say no.

Commitment and Consistency

It is like humans to settle for what is already tried and tested in the mind. Most of us have a mental image of who we are and how things should be. And most people are not going to be willing to experiment, so they will keep on acting the way that they did in the past. So, to get them to work with this principle and do what you want, you first need to get them to commit to something. The steps that you would need to follow to get your target to do what you want through commitment and consistency include:

- Start out with something small. You can ask the target to do something small, something that is easier to manage the change before they start to integrate it more into their personality and get hooked on the habit.
- You can get the target to accept something publicly so that they will feel more obligated to see it through.

- Reward the target when they can stick to the course. Rewards will be able to help strengthen the interest of the target in the course of action that you want them to do.

Social Proof

This is another one that will rely on the human tendency, and it relies on the fact that people place a lot of value and trust in other people and in their opinions on things that we have not tried yet. This can be truer if the information comes from a close friend or a person who is perceived as the expert. It is impossible to try out everything in life and having to rely on others can put us at a disadvantage. This means that we need to find a reliable source to help us get started. A manipulator may be able to get someone to do something by acting as a close friend or an expert. They can get the target to try out a course of action because they have positioned themselves as the one who knows the most about the situation or the action.

Influence is a powerful, but an often subtle tool. The ability to affect or change someone's opinion, or create a change in circumstances without forcing the change directly is an art form all its own. Creating changes or conditions as situations develop creates a lasting impact. It can make others sit up and take notice of you and your presence and often create a perception of you that may make others want to defer to you in the future. We will go over how to create influence, how to build your skills regarding influencing others, and how to utilize the influence you have built to achieve your goals.

Influence is based on basic, but key factors. Let's start with a room full of people whom you do not know. Your entrance into this room is vital. You may not know anyone, but not everyone present will know this. Presenting yourself in the most flattering way within the first few seconds will often dictate the way everyone in the room sees you. Smile as you enter the room, walking with your back and head in straight but relaxed alignment. Taking time not to rush or enter too slowly, imagine you are just walking into a room in your home. An often-effective trick to make you seem more approachable is to give a short wave as if you are acknowledging someone you know. This makes others assume thatsomeone else in the room already knows you and that in and of itself makes you seem more likable or interesting.

When first meeting someone, making eye contact and firmly shaking their hand while smiling boosts your effective charisma with the other individual. Charisma is more about how you make the other person feel when they are in your presence. Charisma is not necessarily about being the life of the party. To work on your charisma; first, consider your own strengths. Are you humorous? Are you already outgoing and friendly? Do you tend to be shy and quieter? You can use any of your strengths to your advantage; it is all about understanding how to use them. If you are more of an introvert, pick one or two people off to the side of the crowd or room to engage with. When initiating communication, use your quieter presence to let others do more of the talking, and only steer the conversation in the direction you want it to go in when necessary. People love to talk about themselves! If you are outgoing, place yourself in a position of power, feel free to approach larger groupings of people, and greet them. Again, use your strengths to your advantage.

People that hold sway over others can attest, influence is all about give and take. When people feel a relationship is based on reciprocation, they trust the relationship easier and sooner and have fewer reservations. Try asking a small favor of someone, and then, in turn, offering them the same in return. An example would be offering to hold someone's place in line while they use the restroom, taking notes for them while they excuse themselves momentarily during a meeting or presentation, and then asking them to do the same for you upon their return. This 'give and take' lays a foundation of comradery, like you and the other party is already friendly. And people that feel like you like them, like you in return.

Building relationships overnight is not easy, but it can be easier by being friendly. Smiling and eye contact play a role in how you make other people feel. If you project that you are happy to see others that you are happy to be speaking with them, they will, in turn, feel happy to be communicating with you. Your body language speaks volumes, and others pick up on what you are conveying with yours, even if they aren't fully aware of it. When engaging with another, take note of how they are standing or sitting. If they are standing with their arms at their sides, you should mimic their stance. Mimicking someone's body language is another way of building an unspoken but solid foundation. If they are clearly exhibiting stress, mimic their stance. An example of this would be if their arms are crossed over the front of their body in a defensive pose. After a few minutes of conversation, move your arms to a more relaxed and natural position. In most instances, the person you are communicating with will subconsciously reposition their body language to mimic your own. This is an example of how you are already gaining influence and trust with someone you barely know.

When talking to individuals you want to gain influence over, another aspect to consider is your own attitude towards them. We know that our physical body language plays a role, and that reciprocating is important as well, but just as important is how you project yourself. Greeting another with a smile is great, but now that the conversation has started, maintains a neutral but relaxed facial expression. Staying involved and being attentive when others speak again makes them feel good speaking with you. Asking questions per the flow of conversation shows that you are listening to them, and everyone wants to be heard. Being respectful, calm, and diplomatic in your interactions makes you more friendly and approachable. Showing gratitude for their time and being appreciated will encourage others to appreciate your attention and time in return.

Chapter 3: Subliminal Persuasion

In our world, subliminal persuasion is everywhere. You can't watch television, read a magazine, or even go for a drive around town without encountering it. The definition of subliminal persuasion is the use of objects, photos, words, or another means of persuading someone into doing something or putting an idea in their head without them consciously knowing what you've done. A common example of this is advertising. When you see or hear the points made when someone is trying to sell you a product, your mind may think of the product as appealing. You usually won't know that the techniques used in the advertisement itself are the reason you feel like you need their product. Often you wouldn't have bought this item otherwise. Below is an example of how this advertising technique works.

Picture this:

A glass of soda is displayed in front of you, surrounded by warm colors. It is perfectly carbonated, as there is an emphasis on the infinite bubbles working their way to the top of the bottle. As it is being opened, the sound of carbon being released rushes from the bottle. It is a perfect day without a cloud in sight, and golden rays of the sun are shining overhead. The glare of the sun is shining on the pristine glasswork. The drink is so cold in contrast with the warm day that precipitation has formed into fat drops of water that are slowly sliding down the glass and following the way it's perfectly shaped to fit a hand.

As a model brings the drink to their lips, just a drop escapes and slides down her chin and it catches the golden light of the sun as it falls slowly out of the frame. The model's eyes slide closed slowly with pure bliss and satisfaction. The camera zeros in on the muscles of her neck contracting and stretching; and as she puts the drink down, a smile forms on her face.

You might not be in a warm area, nor may you particularly want a soda right now. However, that description was followed by your mind and you may feel thirstier than before you read it. This is because my words used subliminal persuasion to make you want the soda that was described. You've seen advertisements like this many times, and they might have worked. Never does a cold drink display so much precipitation as it does on the picture of an advertisement unless it has been sitting in water. However, because the body craves liquid when we are even a little dehydrated, the look will appeal to that natural desire. Even if what your body wants is water, this advertisement will appeal because of the unrealistic water droplets that have formed on the can or bottle.

When using this tactic in the form of manipulating another person, there are a few different ways to go about it. For instance, if you create a sense of "we" and equality in the request, it feels more inclusive. When sales clerks and advertisers work, they often create the idea that the product benefits both them and you as a consumer. They speak as if by buying their product, you not only get the benefit of having the product they think you need, but they will be happier for it.

If you word the request in a form that appeals to both you and the other person, you're more likely to achieve your goal. This form of persuasion can also combine well with cold reading techniques, as both involve the other person believing something without you outright offering the information to them.

Another form of persuasion is gathering favors. Debt is a constant in this world, and it doesn't always mean money. If you've done something for the other person recently, and have earned a form of gratitude, they're likely to feel indebted to you and therefore, more obligated to carry out your request. For example, if you save this person from an embarrassing situation, such as lending them a jacket when they've spilled a drink down their shirt, you may request a favor in return later on. Because you displayed kindness for no apparent reason that they can see, they'll feel the need to retaliate the kindness. Favors can be as large as saving someone's life, or even as small as some good advice. Every act doesn't need to be an all-out sacrifice. It shouldn't be. If someone catches a hint of deception or ulterior motives when someone is displaying such kindness, they will feel distrustful towards you, and you will lose the relationship that you've worked towards by now.

You can use this kind of persuasion technique yourself to get people to do as you wish, provided you do so subtly.

Cold Reading

Cold reading is known to be a con artist's best friend.

It provides the illusion of mind reading and magical abilities without the use of actual supernatural power. It is often used by those who make a living through fortune-telling and psychic acts. Many people have been completely sold on the act, as it is usually performed by someone who excels in reading others, has acquired enough general knowledge, and has practiced enough to deliver a very believable performance.

However, such an act is really only a form of psychology, and you could create this act yourself if you chose to.

You would do this by creating the illusion of knowing more than you really do through the power of observation. There are different names for different techniques. How many people are present decides how you should approach it. Shotgunning, for instance, is done in a large room packed with people. This is often the choice of mediums that are creating the illusion of connecting to a passed loved one because whatever they say, there is likely to be someone who can relate to the statement. When the medium speaks a few, usually vague, phrases, such as "I am connecting to an elderly man... the name John or Jack comes to mind. Does that speak to anyone?" he or she watches for anyone who expresses recognition. The names Jack and John are very common, and many people have lost a grandfather in their time. The medium will then choose one person and watch their face carefully. This is where true psychology steps in. Reading body language is essential to keeping up the ruse, as the medium will need to narrow down the descriptions of the audience members' loved ones.

If, for example, the medium says something about a white picket fence, yet no familiarity comes to this person's face, he or she will have to change their tactic carefully. He or she might explain that he never lived within a white picket fence, but wanted to, or that another relative was also present. If the audience member agrees or seems excited, this medium will know they are getting warmer. This act is continued and even peppered by what are known as "Rainbow Ruses." These are contradictory phrases such as "He was a gentleman; however, he would occasionally display a stern side". Most people have experienced these contradictory moments in their personality; however, the word choice feels so specific thatit seems as if it only applies to the supposed spirit the man or woman is referring to.

Another method of cold reading, which may be more suitable for a smaller population, is to use previous knowledge when observing someone's behavior. This method is often used in detective dramas, as the act is dramatic and exciting to watch, and the character appears intelligent and clever. It is, however, easier than it may appear, as it only takes keen observation skills. For example, if you meet a new person and notice there is graphite smudged along the side of their left hand, you will know that they are left-handed, as those who are left-hand dominant must drag their hand along the previously written words to continue writing.As a left-hander myself, I would know. This phenomenon, which has been jokingly called "The Silver Surfer Syndrome", is an unquestionable indication that this person is left-handed, and youmay say so with confidence as you shake their hand. The confidentstatement will shock this person, and they won't think to look for physical indicators. This can be used as a fun trick to amuse others,or as a shocking factor to carry into a persuasive technique, as those who have recently been surprised don't always think every factor of a decision through.

Cold reading, as any other manipulation tactic, can be used on anyone. And it is. Many people who are studied in the ways of cold reading have used it as a career, such as psychics, fortune-tellers, and any kind of con artist. Such a complicated set-up is not necessary to add this skill to your own toolbox, as you only need your own observation and shock factor. Another example is if you see someone you may already know is a student, you could confidently exclaim that they were studying late and fell asleep on their work as you note the imprint of math work on their left ear.

29

These subtle observations build up over time, and you may gain a reputation with that person. The more you get to know someone, the more background information you will have stored away. For example, say you have a friend named Kyle. Kyle is a single father of an adorable six-year-old girl whom he spends every moment he can. To support her, he works at a grueling desk job where he files paperwork all day long and takes rude phone calls. You know that he likes light coffee with a lot of sweeteners and that he is right-handed.

Today, Kyle arrives with a large coffee in his left hand. You two always meet up every Tuesday at around ten in the morning. Today, it's almost eleven. In the back of his car is a pink hairbrush. When he gets close enough to greet you, you smell the strong aroma of black coffee rising from his cup, and you can see his clothes are wrinkled. Without asking him, what can you deduce from his situation?

I believe that his boss kept him very late and piled on the work the night prior.

He's gotten papercuts before, however even the light touch of his coffee seems to be too much pain this time, so he was working as quickly as he could. Even so, he got home late that night and overslept the next morning. Rushing to get her to school, Kyle likely tossed his daughter's hairbrush back for her to do her best with her hair on their way to school. Due to his exhaustion, he stopped to buy a coffee much stronger than he likes it before meeting with you. Of course, other indicators weren't mentioned in the example. What situations you come to find yourselves observing will vary, as will the indicators that you notice.

Chapter 4: Mind Control Techniques

It's interesting to see that manipulation has been around for a long time, and that is not a new or imaginary concept. Understanding what the art of persuasion is all about is vital to help you to deal with it.

Here, we briefly look at the psychology of manipulation. This allows us to see where it might occur in our lives. It will also help you in identifying those who might attempt to manipulate you. It is not only about people who like to dominate. If we don't know it is happening to us, might be encouraged to act in ways that are incongruous to our normal personality and behavior. Learn how commerce can persuade customers into buying their goods and services. Recognizing such methods will help in dealing with the power of persuasion.

We like to believe that we are individuals who make sensible choices. In our journey of life, we do not always have full control, and we don't always realize this. As children, we are influenced by our parents and have little control over how we are raised. Once in the education system, we are further manipulated. The teachers will tell us all about the social norms and what is expected of us in society. As adults, we are lured in by politicians trying to get their share of votes. Many are persuaded to vote for a party because of what they promise for the future, even if they don't necessarily believe in their policies. This gives such politicians power, and their decisions will affect our lives. Are we in full control of our lives, or are we merely influenced by those who know all the tricks of persuasion?

We will look at how to deal with various manipulative methods, even sometimes covert. First, you need to learn to recognize when you are being manipulated so you can counteract it.

Recognizing the Art of Manipulation

What then, in our everyday lives, do we need to be wary of?

Persuasive Language

The idiom that every picture tells a story is very true. Words can be so much more powerful as they inspire and encourage us, even to the point of manipulation. How many are the time you have been inspired by a good orator who's daring speech motives you into action? The art of words can be so influential in coercing us to believe something, even when our eyes tell us differently. Communication is a powerful tool, especially when it comes to making people do things.

Advertisers and salespeople use language to convince their goods are just what we are looking for. Using words, such as:

Affordable; Easy to use; Safe; Enjoyable; Time Saving; Guaranteed to last.

Note how all these words make us believe they are confident in their products.

Politicians will use language, such as:

- "We" to encompass you in their world.
- "Us" to make you feel a part of a team.

These are all communication tactics to make us feel included, therefore, important.

Bullies use language along with aggressive behavior to achieve their own selfish goals.

Criminal predators, such as psychopaths, sociopaths, and narcissists, are all people who learn the use of persuasive language. This is a means to get their way and gain control over another person.

Techniques Used in Mind Control

Present-day mind control is both innovative and mental. Tests demonstrate that basically by uncovering the techniques for mind control, the impacts can be diminished or disposed of, at any rate for mind control publicizing and promulgation. Increasingly hard to counter are the physical interruptions, which the military-mechanical complex keeps on creating and enhance.

1. Education — It has consistently been an eventual tyrant's definitive dream to "teach" normally receptive youngsters, subsequently, it has been a focal segment to Communist and Fascist oppressive regimes from the beginning of time. Nobody has been increasingly instrumental in uncovering the motivation of present-day instruction than Charlotte Thompson Iserbyt—one can start an investigation into this region by downloading her book as a free PDF, The Deliberate Dumbing Down of America, revealing the job of Globalist establishments in forming a future planned to deliver servile automatons reigned over by a completely taught, mindful exclusive class.

2. Promotions and Propaganda – Edward Bernays has been referred to as the creator of the consumerist culture that was planned principally to focus on individuals' mental self-portrait (or scarcity in that department) to transform a need into a need. This was at first imagined for items, for example, cigarettes, for instance. Nonetheless, Bernays additionally noted in his 1928 book, Propaganda, that "purposeful publicity is the official arm of the imperceptible government." This can be seen most unmistakably in the advanced police state and the developing native nark culture, enveloped with the pseudo-enthusiastic War on Terror. The expanding union of media has empowered the whole corporate structure to converge with the government, which currently uses the idea of promulgation arrangement. Media; print, motion pictures, TV, and link news would now be able to work flawlessly to incorporate a general message which appears to have the ring of truth since it originates from such a significant number of sources at the same time. When one moves toward becoming sensitive to recognizing the fundamental "message," one will see this engraving all over. What's more, this isn't even to specify subliminal informing.

3. Prescient Programming – Many still deny that prescient computer writing programs are genuine. Prescient programming has its causes in predominately elitist Hollywood, where the big screen can offer a major vision of where society is going. For a nitty-gritty breakdown of explicit models, Vigilant Citizen is an incredible asset that will most likely make you take a gander at "amusement" in a unique light.

4. Sports, Politics, Religion – Some may resent seeing religion, or even legislative issues, put together with sports as a technique for mind control. The focal topic is the equivalent all through: isolate and prevail. The systems are very straightforward: impede the common propensity of individuals to participate for their endurance and train them to frame groups bowed on control and winning. Sports have consistently had a job as a key diversion that corrals innate propensities into a non-significant occasion, which in present-day America has arrived at silly extents where challenges will break out over a game VIP leaving their city. Yet, basic human issues, for example, freedom are chuckled away as immaterial.

5. Food, Water, and Air – Additives, poisons, and other nourishment harms modify mind science to make mildness and indifference. Fluoride in drinking water has been demonstrated to bring down IQ; Aspartame and MSG are excitotoxins which energize synapses until they kick the bucket; and simple access to the inexpensive food that contains these toxins, by and large, has made a populace that needs center and inspiration for a functioning way of life. The vast majority of the cutting-edge world is flawlessly prepped for uninvolved responsiveness—and acknowledgment—of the authoritarian tip top.

6. Medications — We can equate this to any addictive substance; however, the mission of mind controllers is to be certain you are dependent on something. One noteworthy arm of the cutting edge mind control motivation is psychiatry, which expects to characterize all individuals by their issue, instead of their human potential. Today, it has been taken to considerably assist limits as a medicinal oppression has grabbed hold where about everybody has a type of confusion—especially the individuals who question authority. The utilization of nerve tranquilizers in the military has prompted record quantities of suicides. To top it all off, the cutting edge medication state currently has over 25% of U.S. youngsters on mind-desensitizing drugs.

7. Military Testing — There is a long history associated with the military as the proving ground for mind control.

8. Electromagnetic Range — An electromagnetic soup encompasses all of us, charged by present-day gadgets of comfort which have been appeared to affect mind work directly. In an implicit affirmation of what is conceivable, one scientist has been working with a "divine being head protector" to instigate dreams by adjusting the electromagnetic field of the mind. Our advanced soup has us latently washed by conceivably mind-changing waves. At the same time, a wide scope of potential outcomes, for example, phone towers are currently accessible to the eventual personality controller for more straightforward mediation.

Mind control is more common than most people think. It is not easy to detect because of its subtle nature. In many instances, it happens under what is perceived as normal circumstances like through education, religion, TV programs, advertisements and so much more. Cults and their leadership use mind control to influence their members and control whatever they do. It is not easy to detect mind control. However, when one realizes it, they can get out and start again.

Chapter 5: Undetected Mind Control

Your mind is your sanctuary. No matter what else can be lost to others, the mind is yours and yours alone. Or so we think. People like to believe that they are the ones in control of their own actions and thoughts. Many times our minds can be susceptible to the influence of others, and this allows others to control our minds if we're not careful.

Think about a time when you watched a horror movie. Your mind and your emotions are already being led and influenced in the movie. All the decisions of the director, from the camera shot, the lighting, and the music can determine how you are going to feel and react. Even though you are in full awareness that you are just watching a movie, the brain is going to respond to the prompts when they are given. If our brain can be so influenced by something that we are aware of, how strong would the influence of a dark manipulator be?

Undetected mind control is often the deadliest type of mind control there is. If someone is already aware that their mind is being influenced, then they have the option to object, either physically, verbally, or mentally. For example, they can choose to avoid any contact with the person who controls them. A lot of people are going to run at the first sign they see a dangerous person trying to get inside the brain and take over. But if the mind controller can get into the brain of their victim without the victim detecting them, then the victim has no chance to put up their defenses before it's too late.

There are going to be two tactics that the manipulator can use to take over the mind of their victim without detection. This includes the use of media and interpersonal interactions. Traditionally, the media mind control was only possible for the larger company. Most individual mind controllers were left to deal with just the interpersonal interactions. But with the changes in technology now, this is no longer the case.

Smartphones and laptops have allowed even individual manipulators to have media mind control. This can make it a very powerful tool that the manipulator can use. While the undetected mind controller is going to be able to use all these methods, they are often going to be more deliberate and only take their actions after some careful consideration. They are sometimes seen as a big more coward compared to some other controllers, such as psychological manipulators, but they will take deliberate actions to find the right victim to do the attack on.

Undetected Mind Control Tactics

Now that we know a little bit more about undetected mind control, it is time to learn about some of the methods that are used by manipulators to control the mind of a victim in an undetected way.

We are going to explore both the media and the interpersonal techniques that are in the toolkit of the manipulator. Let's take a look at some of the different undetected mind control tactics.

Finding Those Who Are in Need

The first principle that comes with undetected mind control is to find a victim who has a goal. It has been proven that a person who has a pressing desire or needs is someone who will be more susceptible to this type of mind control compared to someone that feels satisfied and at ease. This could range from a small physical goal, such as someone thirsty and looking for a drink. Or it can be a more psychological goal, such as someone who is craving affection and love.

A good example of this is the experiment that was conducted to look at a subliminal influence or undetected mind control. In this study, there were two sets of people who were shown a film, but this film had a hidden image of iced tea. One set of people in the study were thirsty, and the second group wasn't.

After the movie, when the participants were given the chance to purchase a specific drink from a selection, the ones who were thirsty would purchase the iced tea in greater numbers compared to those who weren't thirsty. This shows that, when the brain is desperate for something, they are gladly taking suggestions on what they should choose.

So, how would you be able to use this principle with an individual on more of an interpersonal level? If the mind controller can find a victim who is already craving something in their life, then the manipulator will find that it is easier to control that victim. One example is a victim who just got out of a long-term relationship. They may crave the company again and the mind controller would be able to influence their target into thinking that they are the savior for the victim. In reality, they are going to cause harm and even ruin for the victim, but the victim will crave attention so much that they will fall for the mind control that is put on them.

There are a lot of needs that a manipulator is going to seek to exploit their victim, including their need for company, their need to belong, and even monetary stability. These vulnerabilities are going to be exploited by someone who is more experienced for several purposes. They may want to financially or sexually exploit the victim. They may want to gain the victim's allegiance to form a cult or other extreme movement. Some manipulators just go through this process to toy with their chosen victim for their own pleasure.

Media Control with Images

Just like our five senses can be guides in our lives, they can also be our enemies. Our sense of sight is very powerful. This is why we can even dream visually, even when all the other senses are missing, and we can use our sight to see images of past memories.

This can make imagery as well as visual manipulation, a really powerful technique to use with media mind control.

Because of the changes in technology, impactful imagery techniques are in the hands of manipulators all over the place, and they can even take these techniques and tailor them to their specific victims. So, if their victim seems to have a fear or an aversion to something, the manipulator can use the feared images to help access and then warp the emotions of a person without the victim even realizing what's going on.

Let's look at how this type of mind control can work. We are in an age where there are lots of smartphones, videos, and more. Everything is shot in high definition clips and can be sent at fast speeds to someone else. This means that a high-tech manipulator can allude to the feared image. For example, if a manipulative boyfriend knows that his girlfriend has a big fear of insects, they could "accidentally" put a book with a picture of an insect on its cover in the background somewhere during that video chat. While the girlfriend may not consciously register that the book is there, on an emotional and subtle level, she is going to feel the impact.

Restricting Choice

Restricting choice is another form of undetected mind control. It can be a subtle form of this because it is going to provide the manipulator with a range of built-in "get out clauses" if the victim ever starts to get suspicious. The key to this type of mind control is to take away any real choices that the victim has in a specific circumstance, while still providing the illusion that the victim is the one who has the control.

Let's say that there is a woman who is being asked to go out on a date. A regular guy is going to spend some time asking the question and then stammer out an open-ended question. They may say something like "Would you like to go out with me?" This question allows the woman to say yes or no based on their personal preferences. This is the way that people who aren't using manipulation will behave.

But someone who is trying to use mind control will approach all of this differently. They will confidently and smoothly work to charm the victim. They will get that person to laugh a bit and lower their guard. Then, with a lot of confidence and assurance, the manipulator will ask something like "So, am I taking you out on Thursday or Saturday?" This limits the choices that the victim can go with. The answer of no really isn't an option here, so the victim will pick one of the dates they are given. The victim can't really say that they weren't in control, but the manipulator had complete control the whole time.

Now, if the manipulator is caught, or the victim realizes that they are limited on the choices they are allowed to make, the manipulator can backtrack and still look innocent. They could say something to their victim like, "I can't believe you're analyzing my words so much. That really hurts me and makes me not want to open up to you." This can make the victim feel like they were being meant, and they will probably give in.

Media Mind Control with Sound

Sound is another method that the manipulator can use to do mind control. But personal experience and experiments can confirm this. Have you ever had a song that seems to get stuck in your head? How easy did you find it to get that song out of your head? The sound may have had a big influence on you, even though you knew it was there.

The power of audio manipulation is even greater when it is undetected. Experiments have shown that if customers are exposed to music that comes from a specific region, then they are more likely to order wine from that country. When they were questioned about it later, they had no idea that the sound around them was what influenced them for their decision making.

While there are examples of the media mind control with sound in the media and with the government, even individual manipulators can use this kind of mind control as well. One of the creepiest forms of this mind control is to influence the victim when they are asleep subliminally. A skilled mind controller can get their victim when that victim is at the most vulnerable, such as when they are sleeping, and then can implant the dark and devious commands in the ear of their victim. This allows the commands to sink into the lowest layers of the brain of that victim.

Another form of this auditory mind control is to mask the words with other words or noises that sound similar. Sounds that are outside the range of human perceptions can be this type of mind control.

Chapter 6: Brainwashing

What Is Brainwashing?

In the early 1950s, Brainwashing was coined by journalist Edward Hunter, who wanted to describe the Chinese Communists' efforts to control the minds and to think processes of the Chinese people after their takeover in 1949. Brainwashing is a method of controlling or influencing the personal beliefs, thoughts, attitudes, or actions of people themselves to make them believe what they had previously considered to be false. The word "brainwashing" originated from its Nao, the Chinese term which means "washing the brain." Brainwashing is a method by which a person or group makes use of strict austerity measures to influence others to the will of the manipulator. But where does he stop honest persuasion and start brainwashing? Today, there are many forms of persuasion employed, especially in politics. For instance, a simple way to persuade a crowd to follow your instructions is first to state a few things that cause a' yes' response, then add items that are actual realities, and finally, recommend what you want them to do.

Methods

In psychology, the brainwashing study often referred to as the reform of thought, falls into the "social influence" sphere. Every minute of every day, social influence happens. It's the set of ways people can change the perceptions, values, and actions of other people. The enforcement approach, for example, attempts to bring about a change in a person's behavior and is not concerned about his ethics or values. It is the strategy of "Just do this."

Techniques That Are Used in Brainwashing

Isolation

Typically, the first tactic used in brainwashing is to isolate the victim away from his friends and family. They don't have to worry about any third party coming in and questioning what's happening.

Chanting and Singing

Chanting mantras is an essential feature of many religions, notably Buddhism and Hinduism, and nearly every church has some form of hymn-singing adoration. As each church member chants or sings the same words, their voices merge into one song,creating a strong sense of unity and collective identity. That, along with established singing effects such as lowered heart rate and relaxation, could cast the experience of community worship into a positive light. Increased suggestibility is a feature of such a state, and failure to maintain the trance is often followed by the punishment inflicted on cults, ensuring continuous enforcement of ultra-conformist behavior. They added that continuous lectures, singing, and chanting are used by most cults to alter consciousness.

Love Bombing

Cults want to reinforce the feeling that the outside world is threatening and gravely mistaken. In comparison, they also use "love bombing" to make themselves look accommodating. Love bombing means showering with lavish new or prospective hires and displaying attention and affection. The term has probably originated with either the Children of God or the Church of Unification, but can now be practiced in several different organizations. It is a phenomenon of social psychology that we feel strongly compelled to reciprocate other people's kind acts and kindness. It is, so the counterfeit affection, encouragement, and goodwill shown towards initiates by existing cult members are processed to create a growing sense of debt, obligation, and guilt. Margaret Singer called this an essential character of the cult, useful because it's precisely companionship and validation that many new cult recruits are searching for.

The psychologist Edgar Schein claims that people are triggered into a cult through a process of "unfreezing and refreezing. A new cult member starts to reject his old view of the world during the unfreezing stage and becomes open to the ideas of the cults. The cult solidifies this new perspective during refreezing. Schein mentions loving bombing as a critical point of refreezing—recruits who accept the philosophy of cults are rewarded with hugs and compliments but shunned when they ask too many skeptic questions.

Barratrous Abuse

Most cults hire attorneys to prosecute anyone who criticizes them publicly, no matter how trivial the criticism may be. Of course, the cult can usually afford to lose the lawsuits, while ex-cult members are often insolvent after giving the organization's life. Consequently, many ex-cultists are unable to mount an effective legal counterattack. Moreover, due to the ever-present threat of legal action, mainstream journalists are afraid to criticize cult or reference religious material.

Fatigue and Sleep Deprivation

Amway, a multi-level marketing company, has been charged with depriving its distributors of sleep during weekend-long events. It happened because they were including non-stop seminars lasting until the early morning hours, with only brief interludes during which musicians play loud music with lights flashing. A cultivation strategy that is sometimes used in combination with sleep deprivation includes advising participants to adopt special diets that contain low protein levels and other essential nutrients. As a result, the members of the cults will always feel tired, making them powerless to resist the dictates of religious doctrine.

Activity Pedagogy

How does a teacher motivate their students to follow ethical behavior and conformism? The solution is often to integrate some sort of physical exercise or sport into their teaching. Involved in jumping on the spot or running around, and consequently tired, children are less likely to argue or cause trouble. By acknowledging this phenomenon, several cults aimed to have members occupied as a means of control with an endless series of tiring activities. What distinguishes activity pedagogy from mere sports is that the increased mood and group identity experienced after physical activity will be used by a regime or cult to introduce ideological views that could otherwise be met with skepticism. Fatigue by exercise is yet another manner in which the barriers of people can be worn away as a means to enable them to embrace dubious ideas.

Lifton's Process

Robert Jay Lifton, the psychologist, studied former Korean War prisoners and Chinese war camps in the late 1950s. He determined that they would have undergone a multi-stage process that started with attacks on the sense of self of the prisoner and ended with what appeared to be a change of beliefs. Finally, Lifton defined a set of steps involved in the cases of brainwashing which he studied:

Assault on Identity

You're not who you think you believe you are. It is a deliberate assault on the sense of self of a target (also called its identity or ego) and its core system of beliefs. The agent hides everything that makes the target that he is: "You're not a soldier." "You're not a man." You're not protecting freedom. "For days, weeks, or months, the target is under constant attack to the point of becoming exhausted, confused, and disorientated. His convictions in this state appear less reliable.

Guilt

You are wrong. Whereas the existential crisis is setting in, the agent generates at the same time an intense sense of guilt within the target. He attacks the subject repeatedly and ruthlessly for any "sin" committed, big or small, by the target individual. For everything from the wrongness of his beliefs to the style he eats too slowly, he can criticize the target. The goal starts feeling a general sense of shame that all he does is wrong.

Self-Betrayal

Please agree with me you're awful. Once the subject becomes disoriented and submerged in shame, the agent pressures him to condemn his family members, friends, and peers who share the same "wrong" belief system that he maintains (either with the threat of physical damage or of continued mental attack). This abuse of his convictions and of those he feels responsible for heightening the guilt and lack of idea.

Leniency

I can help. The agent gives a small kindness or relief from the violence with the target in a state of crisis. He may offer a drink of water to the target, or take a moment to ask the target what he misses over the home.

Compulsion to Confession

You can help yourself. The target is faced with the comparison between the guilt and pain of identity assault. Then the sudden relief of leniency, for the first time in the brainwashing process, comes. The target may feel a desire to return the favor to the kindness that is shown to him, and then the agent may present the possibility of confession as a means of relieving guilt and suffering.

Challenging of Guilt

It is the reason because you are in pain. After some months of assault, confusion, breakdown, and leniency moments, the guilt of the target has lost all meaning—he's not sure what he's done is illegal, only knows he's wrong. It provides something of a blank slate that allows the agent to fill in the blanks: to whatever he wants, and he can add the remorse, that feeling of "wrongness." The agent attaches the guilt of the target to the creed system, which the agent attempts to replace. The goal comes to believe thatthe source of his guilt is his belief system.

That's not me; that's my attitude. The battled person is relieved to learn that there's an exogenous shock of his wrongness, that it's not himself who's intractably bad—that means he can escape his wrongness by running away from the corrupt system of beliefs. Then he can criticize the people and institutions associated with that system of ideas, and he will no longer be in pain. The goal can free itself from guilt by confessing to actions connected with its old policy of belief. The goal has completed its psychological rejection of its former identity with its full confessions. Now it is up to the agent to offer a new one for the target.

Self-Rebuilding

Progress and Harmony

The agent introduces a new belief system as the path to "good" if you want. At this stage, the agent stops the misuse, providing the target physical comfort and mental calm in combination with the new system of belief. The goal is made to feel it's he who has to choose between old and new, giving the goal the impression that his future is in his own hands. The goal has already abandoned his old belief system in reaction to leniency and abnormality. The choice is not a hard one: the new identity is safe and desirable because it is nothing like the one that has led to its breakdown.

Final Confession and Rebirth

I pick good. The target contrasts the agony of the old with the peace of the new. Then the target individual chooses a new identity, clinging to it as a preserver of life. He rejects his old system of beliefs and promises loyalty to the new one that will make his life better. There are frequent rituals or ceremonies at this final stage to induce the converted target into its new community. Some brainwashing victims have described this stage as a sensation of "rebirth."

Because Lifton and other psychologists have described variations in what seems to be a distinct series of steps leading to a deep state of suggestibility, an interesting question is why some people end up brainwashed, and others don't.

Chapter 7: Covert Hypnosis

This process is also called conversational hypnosis or sleight of mouth. This term is mostly used by advocates of neuro-linguistic programming (NLP). NLP is a pseudoscientific approach to communication and interaction.

The technique's prime objective is to change the person's behavior subconsciously in such a way that the target believes that he changed his mind using his own will. The success of this process lies significantly in the fact that the remains unaware that he was hypnotized or that anything unusual occurred. The focus and attention of the subject are imperative during the conduct of "Standard" hypnosis. This process is identical to salespeople talking to customers when they are tired. This is because critical thinking and questioning of statements require mental effort. The theme of "covert hypnosis" lies in approaching the subject when he is mentally and physically worn out. Covert hypnosis, irrespective of the fact, remains hypnosis. The element of fatigue is incorporated to make the critical thinking process more cumbersome.

Techniques

The notable trait of this process is that the hypnotized individual ultimately engages in hypnotic phenomena in an incognizant manner. There is a striking similarity between Covert hypnosis and "Ericksonian Hypnosis" in that both techniques work to reach deeper levels of consciousness operates by employing covert and subtle means. The surface structure of language then touchesthese more profound levels of consciousness. During covert hypnosis, the hypnotist controls another individual's behavior through establishing.

The subject feels a psychological connection with the hypnotist as he listens to him. The hypnotist, while displaying confidence and control, presents linguistic data in the form of metaphor:

However, it consequently helps in enabling a recovered deep structure of meaning that is directly relevant to the listener.

Put in another way, this process first builds unconscious states within the listener and then connects those states through covert conditioning. This is achieved, for instance, by shifting the use of time and use of identity in language.

An example:

The hypnotist may try to achieve a state of forgetfulness in the subject. This is done when the hypnotist talks with the subject of his feeling in that particular state to gain maximum knowledge about the subject. When the hypnotist discovers that this state is at its heightened peak, he can start talking about that state after this state has attained its maximum peak. That response will be contingent upon the fact that the suggestions were made to draw an immediate effect, and the reader was suggestible enough to be influenced in this way. The core objective of covert hypnosis is to shut down or at least minimize the analytical part of the subject's brain, lest he suspect something. All this may be achieved relatively quickly by an experienced practitioner.

Covert Hypnosis and Media

Real estate expert Glenn Twiddle in June 2010 appeared on the Australian television show A Current Affair. The segment reveals how he teaches real estate agents how to use these tactics on potential property buyers.

Covert Hypnosis in Fiction

Covert hypnosis has been portrayed in television series such as The Mentalist, although somewhat over-represented, the most prominent portrayal of covert hypnosis was in the "Russet Potatoes" episode in which a suspect uses covert hypnosis to manipulate characters in the episode and attempts to kill her boss. Another example of covert hypnosis was in the X-Files, where a man with a tumor in his brain is learning additional hypnosis abilities and using them to escape police captivity.

Learning Covert Hypnosis

If you want to learn covert hypnosis, first, you have to realize that it takes a long time to master properly, but if you practice every day, you will continually see positive results.

When learning how to do covert hypnosis, the difficulty for most people is not their inability to apply the methods, but rather their impatience and ignorance of how covert hypnosis is first and foremost.

There are extremely useful tips given below that will help you learn covert hypnosis.

Get into the Right Learning Mind Frame

It involves understanding how it takes dedication and persistence to master covert hypnosis. When you start learning covert hypnosis first, do not think it's going to be easy.

Covert hypnosis is all about knowing how the human mind functions and discovering how to interact effectively, mentally, and physically, with someone's mind in a subtle way.

While you can learn and apply such methods effectively within a very short space of time, you will not be able to do this effectively to different people without understanding the full processes leading up to that point.

Build Rapport

Many people make mistakes while establishing rapport. Relationship building involves creating a secure connection between the hypnotist and the subject of the hypnotist. The stronger the bond, the more powerful the technique of covert hypnosis is.

The partnership is more than what exists out there. It is an emotional and intense friendship, where people can be inside the minds of each other.

This hypnotic relationship bond is so strong that the subject will see the hypnotist as a figure of authority, and will be more than willing to do what the hypnotist wants them to do with little or no resistance.

Look for Trance Signals

Widening the social awareness networks by increasing the senses is of fundamental importance. It is construed as a critical step as it helps you to see the signs the subject gives as they enter a hypnotic trance.

Recognizing sure trance signs ensures you can move to the next stage of your technique of covert hypnosis.

Recognizing when someone is not hypnotically reacting to you is just as crucial because then you will realize that your manipulation is not working and that you have to find another process.

Understand Hypnotic Language

There is another name for Covert hypnosis, that is, conversational hypnosis, and you need to learn how to practice and sharpen your language skills to make it more hypnotic to influence a conversation.

Whenever you decide and manage to converse in a hypnotic language, it will cause the mind of the subject into a hypnotic state, which you can then influence to respond to in some hypnotic ways.

There is a range of primary and advanced methods in the hypnotic language, and you can do to achieve the hypnotic state of mind, from emotional triggers to manipulating someone's emotions to hypnotic storytelling.

What Hypnosis Is and Is Not

It is essential that you clear from the outset any doubts you have about hypnosis. Hypnosis is presented in the media as a means of total control over another person, and this enormous misconception has affected many people.

Any form of hypnosis won't give anybody complete control over the mind of another. This is just not possible.

Advantages of Covert or Conversational Hypnosis

You are directly influenced by the level of happiness and success of others. If you discover the fundamental secrets of ethical power, the world will be at your feet.

If you don't, you could end up living a quiet, lonely life, just like 95 percent of people who suffer from all kinds of problems needlessly.

Their suggestions and advice do not get much attention. They don't get their due respect. They lose clients and customers, and don't know why!

They are unable to communicate with confidence and have difficulty expressing their proposals to their colleagues. When they meet strangers, they lose their composure and make a poor initial impression.

They cannot get their children to listen and are usually discouraged because things don't seem to be going their way.

But it does get worse!

This is because no one tells you how to be as successful as you grow up. You've just picked up a few things here and there.

Covert Hypnosis Is a Simple Way to Convince People

Another big problem is conventional communications, and it doesn't work out by mere sales training.

You'll see people run away from you if they find you using such techniques.

There's a plethora of proof to suggest hypnosis might just be the answer you've been waiting for. The best part is the right kind of trance, which even works every day during routine interactions. That's okay. If you are talking to someone at a grocery store, at the post office, or elsewhere, you can successfully induce a trance in them. Conversational hypnosis is the technical term for this type of hypnosis.

It is the most potent way of influencing the human mind positively. Over the past 65 years, scientific research has shown that hypnosis can be used secretly. You can create ideas in the minds of people when communicating with them. They are not even going to know it's happening.

Neuro-scientific experiments suggest that all learning behavior and change unconsciously take place in the beginning. Afterward, the conscious mind catches up. So, if you want to be more successful, you've got to reach the people in their unconscious state. This is where the magic transpires.

Hypnosis offers the fastest way to tap into the unconscious mind! Research in the field shows the secret to persuasion is not to try to change people's minds, but to alter their attitudes first. For instance, you must first get somebody in the right mood. Only then can you change their perception and ability to agree with your point of view successfully.

Doctors, psychiatrists, and hypnotherapists have found that: hypnosis opens the mind to suggestion to the point that "normal" mechanisms in the brain can be overridden. At the unconscious level, it works profoundly to create near-instant shifts in hypnotic subjects.

The problem is that regular hypnosis is not possible. You can't walk around, holding a pocket watch, asking people to "look deep into my eyes." Traditional forms of hypnosis are best suited to clinical circumstances. However, you absolutely cannot apply any sort of hypnosis in everyday interactions. If you tried, at best, you will look foolish and outrage people at worst.

The conversational or implicit hypnosis is therefore suitable for typical situations. You can actually hypnotize someone who unintentionally asks for your assistance when chatting over a cup of coffee with them. Covert or conversational hypnosis:

- Is easy to learn, ethical to use, and enjoyable when you perform every interaction.
- Melts vital conscious mind resistance and makes way for easier and faster hypnosis.
- Participants simply don't know they're being hypnotized.
- Activates the suggestibility core of the brain so those thoughts sink into the unconscious mind and take root instantly.
- Creates an atmosphere for bringing someone else in.

Research-Based Evidence on Use and Utility

Since the early 1950s, the American Medical Association has allowed doctors to use hypnosis.

Covert Hypnosis Explained

Covert hypnosis can take many forms. It can be used as a pure and simple form of self-hypnosis, or it may be used to hypnotize another person or group of people.

Whether you choose to hypnotize yourself or another by using conversational hypnotism, the first step you'll want to take is to bring yourself in the desired state.

Getting Ready for Covert Hypnosis

You do not need to learn how to do hypnosis for yourself. Just relax by taking a few deep breaths in through your mouth and letting them out through your nose slowly and gently.

Chapter 8: How to Use Dark Psychology to Succeed at Work

The main reason many people want to learn about darkpsychology is because they want to do it better in their careers. They aren't content working the job they already have: they want to prove themselves to be capable of more.

But somewhere along the way, we figure out the truth: that getting ahead in our careers isn't necessarily a matter of skill, but of manipulation and persuasion. As you know, dark psychology is the best and most legitimate way to learn these skills, and now it's time to learn how to use them specifically in a work setting.

We have to think harder about how we interact with our co-workers. For instance, let's say we have a female early 20-something analyst amid a post-graduation down-cycle who has encountered many challenges both professionally and personally since starting work a few years ago.

She frequently finds herself wanting to connect with people who are perceived to be more advanced in their careers or whose interests are different from her own. Being able to figure out why you are attracted to certain people is a valuable skill for early-career practitioners and likely contributes to her success as an analyst. If she wants to get ahead, she should follow along with all the directions in these pages, where we speak to dark psychology in the workplace directly.

Personality is an especially crucial subject for the context of the workplace because it is an environment where you have to interact with many different kinds of people, many of whom—you will soon find out—you don't actually know that well as people.

Dark psychology is broader than neurolinguistics programming, but NLP is where all of our tools and techniques of deep communication and manipulation come from. NLP is where the three big steps of manipulation and mind control originate from: establish your own state control and perceptual sharpness, imitate the unconscious cues of communication of your subject so that they incorporate you into their mind, and use one of the techniques.

People think constantly without even realizing it because most thought is unconscious. NLP is the way we take advantage of the unconscious nature of most thoughts to tell people's minds to change the structure before they even know it.

The topic of NLP is important for discussing personalities in the workplace because NLP has five main categories for the kinds of personalities people have. In the jargon of NLP, these "personalities" are actually called metaprograms. You would do well to identify the important people at your workplace within these metaprograms. Take advantage of your perceptual sharpness to ascertain this information.

As we have told you before, getting information about the subject is everything. But it is also true that our brains need to sort all the information we get into categories to understand the world better. These metaprograms do that job for you.

Metaprograms are more useful than personalities because they are more objective. They also focus on the motivations people have and the way they use logic, rather than on their mannerisms or less important patterns of behavior. Metaprograms do not simply describe how much you like attention or how nervous or relaxed you are—you may notice some aspects of each metaprogram that overlap with these traits, but metaprograms are much more specific than these less useful terms.

These NLP-styled personalities are not only a way for you to get more information about your co-workers. Remember the second step of NLP mind-reading and manipulation: you have to imitate the cues of communications the subject shows you. When you do this, you make them unconsciously see you as being like themselves. That means if you take on the traits of your co-worker's metaprogram, you make it easier for you to succeed in this step.

The last thing for you to know about metaprograms, in general, is that they are sorted in dichotomies. A dichotomy is a contrast between two items that are different. But while you should choose just one from each dichotomy in each metaprogram, you must remember that people are not as simple as being A or B. Any time we have a dichotomy—in any situation—picking one of the two is just a category you can use to simplify things and think of them differently. But you should not think of them as being always or exclusively one of the two. People are much more complex than this.

Our first metaprogram is between the dichotomy of options and procedures. People who are on the options metaprogram don't like being limited or being told what to do. They want as much freedom as possible, and they like to think about things from a general perspective rather than getting in the weeds. People on procedures, on the other hand, need to understand every small detail whenever they get into something new. Procedures people hate the feeling that there is something they are missing, and when detail is skipped, they fear they are missing something important.

The second metaprogram is external and internal. This metaprogram is concerned with people's incentives. External people want to be told by others when they do good work, and they want to be told when they do bad work, too. Internal people don't want to get outside opinions about their work, though. They feel they know when their work is good or not, and hearing what other people think is just a bother.

The third dichotomy in metaprograms is proactive and reactive. These metaprograms describe how someone deals with the future. Reactive people look at a calendar and are always thinking about how the work they are doing now fits into the picture of all of their work. This can be a hindrance because they think so much about planning ahead that they lose sight of what they are trying to do right now. Proactive people, on the other hand, hate thinking about the future or planning ahead. They only care about the here and now.

Our second-to-last is toward and away. This metaprogram is about goals and deterrents. All of us have things we look forward to in the future, but people are chiefly concerned about their goals, and they don't look behind them at all. Away people are the exact opposite of this. They can have issues looking ahead because they spend so much time thinking about what is behind them.

Finally, we have sameness and difference. Sameness people have a love for familiarity: they spend their time around things they already know. Things they don't know make them fearful, so these people avoid them at all costs. Difference people, on the other hand, are always craving new experiences to have, new people to meet, new foods to eat, and so on. If there is something they haven't experienced yet, different people want to experience it.

These are the five big dichotomies in metaprograms. Whoever the co-worker is who you want to use our dark psychology tricks on; you will want to sort them into these metaprograms. Now, when you use the Aristotelian technique of envisioning the future, you have a more objective stand-in for the person you will interact with.

You see, when we imagine someone in our heads, it isn't always accurate to how they really are. NLP's metaprograms are so useful because they make us think carefully about the kind of person our subject is.

Metaprograms are particularly good for the work environment because they force us to think about the people we work with more objectively. When you do Step 1 and prepare to get into the co-worker's mind with Step 2, you can use these metaprograms to paint a fuller picture of who you are going to use dark psychology on.

Since these are often just people we interact with exclusively in work environments, we can be surprised by how little we might know about them from a metaprogram standpoint. If you are being honest with yourself as you sort them into these dichotomies, you might realize you don't know very much about them at all. When this turns out to be the case, don't just go alongwith the dark psychology technique, anyway. There is no point in doing this when it won't work anyway—you can't adapt to the social cues of a person you don't even know yet.

That's why from here, you will have to do more intel-gathering on them first before you can even move on to Step 1. Step 1 can't successfully happen until you know the person and how they fit into all the metaprograms. Until you do that, you won't be able to properly imagine the interactions you have with them for Steps 2 and 3.

With that said, after you get to know the co-workers' metaprograms, let your senses do all the work in perceptual sharpness, use our exercises to prepare your state control, and imagine the interaction in your imagination, you are ready for Step 2.

For Steps 2 and 3, things go about the same when you are dealing with someone from your workplace. However, some techniques seem tailor-made for use in the work setting. We will go over these before moving onto our big lesson on neurolinguistic programming in psychology.

We will cover three big dark psychology techniques for the workplace before diving into the world of NLP. Social framing is a technique in which we paint a picture for the subject where adopting a certain behavior or idea will help them with social climbing.

Our social lives are one of the most important things to us as humans. That's why framing the truth about the subject's social environment is such a powerful tool for manipulating and mind-controlling people. As long as we make them believe they get a social reward for doing what we say, they will jump at the opportunity.

Executing this technique is simple. Assuming you have already mentally sorted them into the proper metaprograms, controlled your state, and are paying close attention to your senses.

Chapter 9: When "No" Means "Yes"

Have you ever rented a car and been adamant that you didn't want insurance, but somehow walked out with it, anyway? Have you wondered how they got you to believe that you needed something that you didn't want in the first place? There is a sort of power and control within the resounding no. The rental agent already knows that you are going to walk in telling them what you want and don't want. Most people do not want the extra insurance because they have their own insurance and feel like paying extra for more insurance isn't worth it, especially when you probably aren't going to need it. The resounding "no" is so common that it is something salespeople don't even pay attention to anymore. It is an instant reaction that is driven by the fear of getting swindled into doing something that you do not want. So, you walk in already with your mind made up.

However, the rental agent found a way to get you to buy the product still. Think about it, before they even work on your contract, they go outside and walk you around the cars. During this time, they ask you questions about your trip, what you need it for, and then they start telling you about the amenities of the car—that they carry car seats, and they sell you the coverage based on what appeals to you through the conversation you had. You felt like you had a great conversation with the salesperson, but in reality, they were using the time to prey on you because they know what you will need on this trip you are taking and how what they have to offer will alleviate your stress and/or solve your problem.

When changing your audiences' answer from no to yes, it is about understanding how they make decisions, what appeals to them—by testing the waters—how they remember things, and howthey look into the future. Most of the time, people remember important dramatic experiences that turn out badly. The rental agent might ask you if you have car insurance and you tell them that you have what the law requires because you own your car.

This is when they realize that they want to protect their car, but they also want to make you think that they are protecting you from having to pay tons of money out of your pocket. So, they will tell you that they have rental coverage that covers the car bumper to bumper. It is only $11–$14 a day depending on the car size, and there is no deductible. If anything happens to the car, it will be covered, and you will just walk away without paying a dime. This might sound appealing to the customer, but they still feel like they don't need it. So, they tell the rental agent "no" again.

This is when the agent moves to a story to sway the customer. The agent tells the customer they understand how they feel. Telling them that they buy the coverage doesn't help. They need to tell them a story that they will remember, a dramatic one that will sway them to their side. The agent brings up an encounter with a previous customer who felt the same way as the current one. The customer was adamant about not getting the coverage that covered the car and rented the car without it.

Another car ended up hitting them in the parking lot, and they walked back in asking if they could get the coverage. The rental agent had to end the rental contract and not give them the coverage because it is illegal to sell it after the rental agreement has been made and after an accident. The customer ended up paying for the damages out of their pocket, as well as the life of therental in the shop, which means they had to pay the amount of therental up to five days. All because they didn't want to pay an extra $30. Due to this story, the current customer ended up purchasing the coverage that covered the car.

When the agent was telling the story to the new customer, all they remembered was the outcome of the crash in the parking lot. They didn't remember anything else about the story, just that theydidn't want to go through what the previous customer went through.

Covert Persuasion can be used in different situations, especially when you are trying to win and bring them over to your side. In customer service, you want them to talk about your competitor and discuss their past experiences because if they were satisfied with that experience, they wouldn't be talking to you. One of the things that you have to do is make sure that you don't scare them away so that they do not want to purchase from you.

Have them tell you a story of a great purchase experience they had. This helps you from not scaring them off because you are having them remember a fun experience. For instance, if you are a stockbroker and the potential customer is someone who has lost money in the stock market, you will understand why they don't want to risk money again. But isn't that the risk with the stock market? You're not going to make money every time.

The broker has to be careful in this situation, and they cannot guarantee the potential customer or investor that they will not lose money again. That will be a lie, and that will break their trust right there. The broker has to point out that it is a possibility that they would lose money again. However, it is more likely that they will get typical returns with their investment.

Persuasion research is very clear, especially with covert persuasion. The speaker must show the audience both possible outcomes for them to be successful. If the speaker doesn't indicate that the investor might lose money in the stock market, they will continue to be afraid of it and choose not to invest with your brokerage firm.

When you show them that losing money is a possibility, you also show them what else could happen within reason. If you make it sound too good to be true, the possible investor will feel like they are being manipulated, and they will still choose not to go with your firm's offer. By keeping it realistic, there is a high chance that they will succumb to your persuasions.

Be clear with your message delivery. If the possible investor lost the first half of the game, they need to come in strong during the second half. Never let what happened in the past determine what they could possibly achieve in the future.

The whole idea of persuading people is to take away their fear of saying yes, which is normal. People tend to have a fear of the unknown and how their life will change. If you are trying to help someone quit smoking, the person will resist at first because the fear of deterring from their normal routine is too much for them. To help them overcome this fear, you will have to substitute their current fear with one that is far worse. Basically, you are scaring them beyond their worst fears. For instance, the speaker tells the person that if they continue to keep smoking every day that it is going to cause you to die. Can you imagine your kids and grandkids standing over your casket? They will remember you theway you looked in that casket. The idea of their family looking overtheir dead body scares them, especially when it is something that they could have prevented. This is when the speaker makes the fear less painful by helping them cut down. Tell them to start smallby cutting down to half a pack a day this month, then only one every day next month and by the next month, you don't need them anymore. Wouldn't it be great to show your family that you don't need to smoke? Wouldn't it be great to show them how healthy you are?

The speaker used fear to persuade the person to stop smoking and then gave them a set of instructions that will help them with the new decision that they made. The person was able to see how changing their life and going with what you wanted wasn't hard if they worked at it. They weren't going to be worse off because of the decision, but better.

So, once the speaker can change or is persuaded to do what you want them to do, they should be happy that they listened to you and took your advice—whether it is to change their attitude or behavior or purchase what they are selling. This is not always the case, though.

There is a principle known as option attachment. Someone has a choice to purchase one of two puppies. Either puppy would be a good pet for her, but each one is different. They ponder which puppy they could see themselves keeping, and no matter which one they choose, even though they are not aware of it, they worry that the other puppy will be the better of the two because the person did not choose them.

Wouldn't they feel good about the choice they made? You would think that they would be happy, relieved, or even comfortable with their decision. Yet, they are miserable. They start to question the decision that they made.

When someone is left thinking about their options too long, they tend to think that whatever they choose; they are losing something by not choosing the other thing. The initial problem is the choice they are left with. The person feels a sense of disappointment and loss when they realize that they have to let the other option go.

Persuasion research indicates that it doesn't matter if the person has personally experienced both options set in front of them, or just imagining one. Whatever option they choose, the other one becomes more attractive because they cannot have it.

The second factor of option attachment is the feeling of loss. The person felt attached to the other option when they were deliberating.

There are two ways to help counteract option attachment:

1. Don't let the person feel any sort of attachment to both of the options. You don't want them to feel a sense of loss. So, make sure that they don't have a lot of time to make the decision. Tell them that the decision has to be fast.

2. If you have to give them more than one option, make the better option more attractive to them so that they do not spend a lot of time making a decision. Don't let them feel connected with

something they are never going to have. Give them info about the option and then make them understand why it is not feasible.

Conclusion

Persuasion is a process of modifying and reconstructing an individual's opinions, beliefs, values, and behaviors to obtain a result. People are programmed to find it extremely difficult to get out of their comfort zone, regardless of their comfort zone. For some people, even if their comfort zone is not very healthy, they would not mind staying in it because, well, it is comfortable.

Persuasion is not about forcing an individual to behave the way we want them to behave; it is about allowing them to step out of their comfort zone to reach a higher comfort zone after the discomfort of the change diminishes. Simply put, an individual who habitually smokes will continue to smoke because it is their comfort zone. Persuading or convincing them will be a great challenge because quitting smoking is an uncomfortable task for the person. During the non-smoking period, this person may experience considerable discomfort. However, later on, they will experience a greater comfort zone due to the lack of their unhealthy behavior.

CPSIA information can be obtained
at www.ICGtesting.com
Printed in the USA
BVHW040347190521
607637BV00005BA/894

9 781801 919708